HOW TO START YOUR OWN
PHONE SEX BUSINESS

Makaila Renee

An Original Kaila's Playhouse Edition
BALTIMORE, MARYLAND

An original **Kaila's Playhouse** Edition
Baltimore, Maryland 21201

Copyright © 2010 by Makaila Renee

ISBN 13: 978-1482065374
ISBN-10:1482065371

First Kaila's Playhouse printing- January 2013

Manufactured in the United States of America

Cover design by Nathaniel Curry

TABLE OF CONTENTS

A BRIEF INTRODUCTION

This book contains a variety of resources for starting your own phone sex business in less than 30 days. This book also serves as an official guide on how to become a successful phone sex operator. After following the 5 simple steps in this book, you will have your own phone sex business up and running in no time at all, GUARANTEED! Before you begin, you must first ask yourself:

Is Phone Sex For You?

Are you a sexual person or at least capable of unleashing your inner sexual being? If not, this may not be the right industry for you. Let's face it- sex sells! When you turn on your television or go to the local movie theater, you will see that sexual images and innuendos are prevalent. Even in a declining economy, phone sex business owners still continue to earn substantial revenue with proper advertisement and promotion.

To discover whether or not the phone sex industry is for you or if you could become a successful phone sex operator, feel free to take the Phone Sex Operator Assessment Quiz on page 23.

STEP 1:
Choosing Your Phone Number

The first thing you must do to start your own phone sex business is to *wisely* choose a phone number. This number must be uniquely selected for your phone sex chat line and should *NOT* be your home phone number or cell phone number. Using your personal home or cell phone numbers may be dangerous if it gets into the wrong hands. In the phone sex business, you are only selling a fantasy. People who have a hard time separating fantasy from reality may utilize your personal home or cell phone number to stalk or harass you. As a former phone sex business owner, I cannot stress the need of a separate and unique number for your business enough.

Keep in mind- you can always obtain a business phone number and have the calls forwarded to your home or cell phone, if you insist on taking calls from your cell phone.
There are several ways to obtain a phone number for your business. The best option is to go to www.chooseanumber.com. This service will assign you with a toll-free number or give you the option to select a vanity number for your business. Here are a few sample numbers for your phone sex business line:

800- 55- GIRLS
877- 555- SEXY
866- 555- FUCK… and so on.

800 vs. 900 Phone Numbers

Choosing the right 800 or 900 number for your business is important and you don't have to be a brain surgeon to do it. The main difference between the two is on how the customer will be billed.

With a 900 number, customers receive a bill via their telephone carrier, meaning that the call will be added to the caller's monthly phone bill. With an 800 number, customers must enter their credit card number and be billed before the call is transferred to you.

The pros and cons of choosing a 900 number is that customers that call your phone sex line don't have to scurry to find their credit card information. The downside to a 900 number is that customers may later dispute the charge(s) on their telephone bill, resulting in a refund or nonpayment of services that have already been rendered. Although this is rare, nobody wants to take 10 calls, only to be paid for 8 because 2 callers have contacted the phone company to dispute the charge to their phone bill.

On the other hand, an 800 number will bill directly to the callers credit card. These charges are harder to dispute because the caller has manually entered their credit card information. In addition, the 800 number is toll free and can be accessed worldwide, without paying any long distance fees. The downside to choosing the 800 number could be that the caller may not want his/her spouse to see the charges on their credit card statement.

Using a Local Phone Number

Using a local number for your phone sex business can be a good choice if you only plan on servicing callers from your local area. However, if you would like to expand your reach, your best bet is to choose an 800 or 900 number for your business line. If you live in California, callers in Tennessee of New York may not want to endure the long distance charges in addition to the actual cost of the call. You can contact your local telephone service carrier and speak to them about an additional phone line, if you choose this option, or simply Google 'Get a Business Phone Number' for a list of service carriers.

STEP 2:
Setting up Your Personal Phone Sex Line

Setting up your personal phone sex line is the most important step in starting your phone sex business. In this step, you should do as much research as possible to find the best telephone service plan for you. Services like Vonage offers per minute plans, meaning that you will pay a certain number of cents for each minute that you are speaking with a client. For example, if you charge $3.99 per minute for phone sex, and you pay $0.09 per minute for phone services, then your net profit would be $3.90.

Other service carriers like Grasshopper offers packages with a set amount of minutes per month for a fixed price. Let's say you've chosen the 'Ramp' package which offers 500 minutes for $24/month. This is great if you only receive a few calls per week, but if you go over your 500 minutes, you will be charged six cents or more for each additional minute.

With so many telephone service options, how can you choose? In my experience, the best route is to choose a company that offers a fixed monthly rate with no contract for service and offers unlimited minutes. PayPerCall.com is a great company that offers unlimited minutes for a flat fee of about $50 a month.

PayPerCall also offers both 800 and 900 numbers to customers and handles billing, as well.

Selecting Phone Service Tip:

In a growing business, I find it easier to select a telephone service company that has the capabilities of handling billing solutions. This leaves you available to handle the more important aspects of the business, such as employee management (if you plan on having employees), advertising and promotions.

STEP 3:
Payment Options

Most phone sex companies except payments from clients/callers via third parties or directly. With a third party (as discussed in the 800 vs. 900 Numbers section of this book), the caller's credit card or phone bill is automatically billed and monies are then sent to you via paper check or direct deposit.

You also have the option to collect your own money. PayPal's Virtual Hosting account provides a way for you to collect your customer's credit card information over the phone or you can send your customer an invoice via email. Contact PayPal or visit www.PayPal.com to set up your account or for more information about Virtual Hosting.

STEP 4:
How to Be a Successful Phone Sex Operator: Getting to Know Your Phone Sex Characters

The key to becoming a successful phone sex operator lies in getting to know your phone sex characters. Below is a list and description of the most common phone sex characters to help you get started.

Commonly Used Characters

1. Barely Legal: Barley Legal's character is 18 or 19 years old. She is a High School student or a recent graduate with big firm tits. She may be immature and playful, but she's *always* horny and willing to do *anything* to please…
2. The MILF: The MILF character is between 30-45 years old. She is sexually experienced and very sensual. She's generally a hot stay-at-home mom who can't wait for her husband to go out of town so she can phone fuck you. This is a very dirty lady.
3. Asian Girl: The Asian character may be small and petite, but is packed with a lot of pleasure. What really drives men crazy about this character is her small size and her exotic accent. She can be any age over 18.

4. Black Girl: The African American character
    must have an ample ass, unlike the other
    characters. Doggy style is usually her favorite
    position, as men love to grip or stare at her ass
    during intercourse. She is one of your most
    sexual characters and loves to talk dirty. She can
    be any age. WARNING: If you are not African
    American, don't try to force an accent or you
    may just make yourself sound stupid! Instead,
    you should just be yourself since all Blacks
    speak with different dialects anyway. Your
    physical description of Black Girl will be more
    than enough to excite the caller.

5. Spanish Girl: The Spanish Girl character, like
    Asian Girl is heavily reliant on the accent,
    which drives men wild. This hot and spicy
    Latina is very sexual and knows exactly what to
    say and do to please her man. She generally has
    dark exotic features and big tits. Like Black
    Girl, she has a high sex drive and loves to fuck.
    She can be any age.

6. Chick with Dick: Chick with Dick is pretty self-
    explanatory. This character has had all of the
    work done to become a woman except one
    thing. She still has a big cock under her tight
    skirt! The freakiest of all of your characters,
    Chick with Dick can be any age.

The Art of Acting: Phone Sex 101

Do you enjoy sucking cock? Maybe you don't, but, as a phone sex operator you absolutely love it! Phone sex combines the art of *acting* with the art of *storytelling*. You will need to develop the ability to do both if you want to become a successful phone sex operator! After getting to know your characters, practice using them on your partner or a close friend. Another way to prep for success as a phone sex operator is to call a phone sex line and just listen to what the operator on the line is saying. If you don't think your quite ready to open your own business, but still want to be a phone sex operator for someone else's company, visit www.SexyJobs.com for a listing of hiring companies.

STEP 5:
Promote and Advertise Your Business

Advertising and promoting your business is the second most important step, next to setting up your actual phone sex service line. If you do not advertise your business, then how will people know to call you for services? They won't. The best ways to advertise your company without spending money is to utilize free online tools like Facebook, YouTube and Twitter to advertise your services.

It is also important to create your own personal website to attract customers to your site. Go to www.MakailaGrant.com/websites to get your own personal website for only $200. Makaila Grant Productions specializes in building small business websites and can have your site up and running in two business days. They also work closely with clients to determine the overall look and needs of the site. Trust me, without a website, you may as well be invisible.

The media can also be a helpful tool in business advertising and promotion. If you can afford television and/or radio advertising, great! If not, try putting an ad in local papers or magazines to draw attention to your business. Advertising on sites like Craigslist or Backpage may be equally helpful in promoting your business.

Phone Sex Operator Assessment Quiz

0 = Not at all
1 = A little
2 = Fairly
3 = Yes or Very much

Based on the key above, please answer the following seven questions truthfully and honestly to assess your success as a phone sex operator.

A.   Are you comfortable with your sexuality? 0 1 2 3

B.   Are you comfortable with talking dirty? 0 1 2 3

C.   Are you a good storyteller? 0 1 2 3

D.   Have you ever been interested in acting? 0 1 2 3

E.   Do you enjoy love stories (books or films)? 0 1 2 3

F.   How liberal do you think you are? 0 1 2 3

G.   If you were a phone sex operator, could you openly share this with your friends and family? 0 1 2 3

Results of final score:

18- 21= You would make an excellent phone sex op!

14- 17= You are likely to be a successful phone sex op!

 7- 13= You need to step your game up!

6 or Less= This is definitely not the right job for you!

4146133R00015

Printed in Great Britain
by Amazon.co.uk, Ltd.,
Marston Gate.